IF IT HAS TO BE ITS UP TO ME

Hardik H. Rane

qurate
quratebooks.com

If It Has To Be Its Up To Me
Hardik H. Rane

Published in 2026

© Published by

Qurate Books Pvt. Ltd.
Goa 403523, India
www.quratebooks.com
Tel: 1800-210-6527, Email: info@quratebooks.com

ISBN: 978-93-58983-66-1

Foreword

I have known Hardik for the past six years. When I first met him, he was a curious 16-year-old with an eagerness to learn and explore new ideas. From the very beginning, I observed in him a rare combination of curiosity, dedication, and a strong work ethic qualities that set him apart at such a young age.

During our time working together at Junior Chamber International (JCI) India, Hardik consistently demonstrated exceptional commitment and enthusiasm. His efforts were recognized on an international level when he won awards in public speaking competitions, an achievement that speaks volumes about his confidence, clarity of thought, and communication skills.

I have always seen him actively engaging in various pursuits traveling, participating in events, contributing to social activities, and balancing his academic responsibilities with remarkable discipline. Keeping oneself meaningfully engaged at such a young age is truly commendable, and Hardik embodies this spirit beautifully.

When he told me that he had written a book, I was both surprised and excited to read it. As I began going through its pages, I was deeply impressed by the depth of his knowledge and the maturity of his insights. This book is a thoughtful guide for anyone seeking purpose, inner strength, and clarity in life. It gently reminds us that we should not wait for miracles, but instead take consistent action toward our goals.

One of the most distinctive aspects of this book is how it incorporates teachings from the Bhagavad Gita, explained in a simple and relatable manner. This makes the book not only inspiring but also spiritually enriching. The narrative is engaging and compelling. You will find it difficult to put the book down until you have finished it.

I wholeheartedly wish Hardik great success for his book, If It Has To Be, It's Up To Me, and all his future endeavors. May he continue to inspire many more lives with his passion and wisdom.

Mrs. Shruti Gaurish Parabdesai
Teaching Professional,
Social Worker & Freelance Content Writer

Acknowledgments

Like all books, *If It Has To Be, It's Up To Me* is the culmination of the unwavering support and guidance of countless individuals. While it is impossible to name everyone who helped me along the way, I wish to express my deepest gratitude to a few who have been particularly instrumental in bringing this vision to life.

To my Grandparents, to whom this book is dedicated: your solemn and steadfast support has always been my foundation.

To Papa, Mummy, Vinay Kaka and Kaki, Suraj Kaka and Kaki, Bindesh Kaka, and my neighbourhood Chachi: thank you for believing in me. Your endless support has never once wavered.

A profound note of gratitude goes to my professor, Dr. Sudhir Sir. During one of the most challenging phases of my life, you looked me in the eye and told me to just travel, reminding me that the sky is the limit. Your advice to always keep working and doing good became the anchor that kept me moving forward.

To Dr. Rakesh Kumar Sir, who first saw my potential and told me I could write. Your motivation was the original spark of this entire project.

To Dr. Anushka Botelho Ma'am, my senior, who patiently guided me through every line of this manuscript.

To JC Shruti Parab Ma'am and Veda, whose early assurance that these words carried weight gave me the final confidence I needed to share them with the world.

A special thank you to Dev Sir, Rishikesh, and Rimjim for your creative vision and invaluable guidance in perfectly capturing the essence of this book through the cover design.

To my roommates and two absolute gems, Vedang and Pushpraj: thank you for constantly pushing me forward whenever the comfort zone seemed too inviting.

To all my friends both from childhood and college along with my relatives and well-wishers, your continuous support has been invaluable.

Finally, to everyone who reads, listens, and dares to believe: Thank you.

Prologue

Back at eighteen, I told myself I had a plan,

To write a book by twenty-two and show it to the man.

But I never felt eligible, I never felt ready,

My mind was too heavy and my hands weren't steady.

But today I got two months left on the clock,

And I'm staring at a door that I gotta unlock.

I got struggles in my mind, but I don't give a damn,

Because the failure and the mess is exactly who I am.

From the day I started dreaming to the day that I fell,

I walked through the heaven and I walked through the hell.

I see all twenty-two years of the ups and the downs,
I see the fake smiles and I see the real frowns.

And I realized I got nothing to lose but my hope,
So I'm done trying to cope, I'm cutting the rope.

I am here before you, leaving nothing behind,
Just the raw, honest story of a messy mind.

But don't get it twisted, I didn't lose the fight,
I found a way to turn the darkness into light.

This isn't just a story of a boy who fell,
It's how to build a heaven when you're going through hell.

So trust in the journey and trust in the flow,
I'm planting the seeds and I'm watching them grow.

From the heavy heart to the spirit that's free,
This is the person I was born to be.

- Hardik Rane

Contents

Introduction

The Ink and the Unknown

We are all handed a script the moment we are born. We are told how to act, what to study, and what kind of "social tags" we need to wear to be considered successful.

We are all walking around wearing invisible tags. The Good Student. The Future Doctor. The Responsible Son.

But what happens when you hit a speed breaker so hard that it derails the entire plan? You get a choice. You can either let the societal tags suffocate you, or you can finally drop them and figure out who you actually are.

For a long time, I watched people around me blindly follow that script, grinding through their daily routines, completely undecided about what they actually wanted out of life. But when I was a 17-year-old boy, a different kind of dream started keeping me awake. I didn't want to just follow the routine; I wanted to write. I wanted to understand the world, figure out my own mind, and put it all down on paper. I realized early on that the comfort zone is a beautiful place, but absolutely nothing ever grows there. This book is the result of that 17-year-old's dream.

It is the raw, unfiltered journey of a guy in his twenties who had to break down before he could break through. Over the next twelve chapters, I am not going to give you generic, textbook advice. Instead, I am going to take you with me.

Over the next twelve chapters, I am taking you on a massive, unfiltered journey. We will dive into the spiritual chaos and profound clarity of the Mahakumbh. We will break down the 6 phases of meditation, diving deep into what it actually takes to understand your true self and find your own inner stillness. We will pack our bags, ignore the logic, and travel straight to the freezing, snow-capped peaks of the Himalayas alongside day-one childhood friends.

And finally, we will talk about what it takes to stand on an international stage, wearing a crisp suit and boots, realizing a vision that started with a simple, quiet thought in a seventh-standard auditorium.

I wrote this because I want you to know that the world is full of possibilities, but nobody is going to hand them to you. You don't need to have it all figured out right now. You just need your hands, a dream in your heart, and the courage to step into the unknown.

Once you decide you want to have a good life, life will actually start getting good. If you are ready to drop the tags, pack your bag, and finally meet the real you—turn the page. Because if it has to be, it's up to me. And now, it's up to you.

❋❋❋

Chapter - 1

The World in the Mirror

We often walk through life under the impression that we are merely reacting to the world around us. We think that if we could just change our circumstances get better marks, win a medal, or receive the applause of a crowd then we would finally feel "right" on the inside.

But the truth is much more profound: the world around us is a reflection of the world within us. Every tendency we see outside whether it is the quiet confidence of a leader or the paralyzing fear of a beginner is actually rooted in the architecture of our own minds and hearts. This isn't just a motivational idea; it is a divine mystery of how we live. If we can change the interior, the exterior begins to shift in response. But to understand the reflection in the mirror today, I have to take you back to the day the glass first cracked.

The Day the Music Stopped

I learned the power of the mirror the hard way. In the 6th standard, I stood on a stage, gripping a microphone with palms that wouldn't stop sweating. My heart wasn't just racing; it felt like it was trying to escape my chest. I opened my mouth to speak, and my voice simply cracked.

The crowd laughed. It wasn't a malicious laugh, but to a young boy, it sounded like thunder. I walked off that stage feeling defeated, convinced that I was fundamentally flawed. I spent a long time wondering if I could ever be "one of those" people the confident ones, the capable ones. I had let a single moment define my entire self-image. I had looked into the mirror and decided that what I saw was a failure.

The First Spark: The 9th Standard Turning Point

Growth doesn't always start with a grand realization; sometimes, it starts with someone else's belief in you when your own has run dry. In the 9th standard, three years after I had vowed never to touch a microphone again, a teacher saw something in me that I had hidden away. She gave me a chance not just to speak, but to heal.

I remember standing on that school stage. Above me hung a banner that read "STAND STRONG." It felt like a direct challenge from the universe. I took a deep breath, and for the first time, the words came out with a clarity I didn't know I possessed. I wasn't just reciting lines; I was discovering a part of myself. That day, I didn't just win a moment of applause; I won back my confidence. The reflection in the mirror had begun to change.

The First Spark: A quiet beginning where I first

learned that a trembling voice could still speak a powerful truth.

The Path of the Silent Worker

That single experience in school became the foundation for everything that followed. I didn't become a speaker overnight; I became a student of the craft. I started seeking out every opportunity, every small stage, and every local platform I could find. Each milestone was a brick in a new foundation. I represented my school, then my district, and eventually, I found myself representing at levels I once thought were reserved for "other" people.

I began to realize that speaking wasn't about the volume of my voice, but the sincerity of my intent. The more I worked on my inner world the more I read, reflected, and meditated the more the outer world seemed to open its doors. I wasn't chasing success; I was building a person that success could finally recognize.

The Evolution: Under the Blinding Lights

This quiet, consistent work eventually led me to a moment that felt like a dream. By the 12th standard, the boy who once feared a classroom audience was standing under the blinding, professional lights of a national television reality show.

Standing on that set, I felt a deep sense of humility. I wasn't there because I was special; I was there because I had been a faithful student of my own journey. I represented my roots, my journey, and the people who believed in me on a global stage. This led to further invitations to speak on national and international platforms, where I was honored to be known as a "good speaker."

But to me, that title was never a trophy. It was a responsibility. Whether I was speaking in a small hall or being broadcast to millions on Daijiworld TV, Dhoordharshan TV the mission remained the same: to be a bridge between the lessons I had learned and the people who needed to hear them. The journey from a local classroom to an international stage was simply proof that the mirror always catches up to the vision—if you are willing to do the work.

A reminder that the biggest stages are built in the quietest hours of internal growth.

Planting Better Seeds

What I didn't realize then is that our thoughts are seeds. After that failure, I was planting "weeds": You're not good enough. What if you fail? Others are way ahead of you. These thoughts are invasive; if you don't remove them, they take root. But growth is a choice. I began to observe the speakers I admired. I realized that they weren't fearless; they just had a desire to grow that was louder than their fear of failing. I started taking tiny, shaky steps. I celebrated the small wins like just showing up on days when I felt like hiding because I realized that big things are built on small, quiet efforts.

Who is Running the Show?

Every day, we have to ask ourselves: Who is doing the thinking inside me? Is it the Fearful Doubter who remembers the 6th-grade crack? Or is it the

Dreamer who remembers the 9th-grade spark? Whomever we choose to "feed" is the version of us that will grow.

You don't need the world's permission to grow. You don't need a medal to prove you're worthy. You just need to believe in the person in the mirror and take the next step forward. Because when your inside gets stronger, your outside becomes unstoppable.

Reflect and Realign

Take a moment to be intentional with your own journey.

1. Define Yourself: You are not your marks, your mistakes, or your medals. Who are you from within?

2. Choose Your Action: Start small. Action beats overthinking every single time.

3. The Mirror Exercise: Take a deep breath and write down the following:

    - I will STOP doing: (A negative thought or habit you are removing).

- I will START doing: (A small step toward growth).
- I will CONTINUE doing: (A positive behavior you want to maintain).

❋❋❋

Chapter - 2

Let It Hurt, Then Let It Go

Those who do amazing things in life aren't the ones who never saw darkness. They are the ones who have been through the storms, the heartbreaks, and the failures but instead of staying there, they chose to focus on the next light rather than the last shadow.

The Weight We Carry

Letting go isn't about forgetting what happened; it's about choosing not to carry it anymore. We often mistake holding on for strength. We think that by gripping our pain tightly, we are somehow honoring what we lost or protecting ourselves from being hurt again. But the truth is, true strength lies in the release.

Don't burn your present trying to fix a past that is already gone. When we hold onto old wounds, we aren't just remembering them; we are punishing ourselves with them. This is where Radical Forgiveness comes in. You don't forgive the person who hurt you for their sake you do it for your own peace. You cannot heal while holding onto poison.

My Story: Choosing Growth Over Bitterness

There was a time I thought letting go meant losing, as if I were giving up on something I cared about deeply. In college, I had someone I truly valued. We shared conversations but eventually, the warmth was replaced by misunderstandings and betrayals.

I tried to fix it. I gave more than I had left to give, until one day I realized: I was holding onto pain and calling it friendship.

The day I decided to let go wasn't the day the hurting stopped it was the day the healing began. I didn't wait for an apology that was never coming. Instead, I took charge of my life. I started playing sports again, I traveled, and I began winning competitions. I wasn't doing it to prove anything to anyone else; I was doing it to rebuild the self-respect I had lost.

That focus saved me. It reminded me that I was not a person who had been broken; I was a person who was becoming. Letting go didn't mean I stopped caring; it meant I started caring about myself more.

The Two Monks and the Burden of the Mind

There is an old story about two monks who were traveling together. They came to a river where a young woman was struggling to cross. The senior monk, without a word, picked her up and carried her to the other side.

Hours later, the junior monk, who had been brooding in silence, finally burst out, "How could you do that? You know our vows forbid us from touching women!"

The senior monk looked at him and replied, "I set her down at the riverbank hours ago. Why are you still carrying her?"

This is what we do. We don't carry people physically, but we carry their words, their actions, and their memories in our minds. Peace begins the moment you decide to put that burden down.

This is a quiet morning in my village. Me standing on that boat in the river, watching the sun rise over the hills that have seen me grow, I had to make a choice. I realized that the river doesn't hold onto yesterday's current, and I couldn't keep holding onto yesterday's hurts if I wanted to reach that new light. Sometimes, the most important journey is the one where you just look forward and decide to put the past down.

The Flowchart of Freedom

How long will you let someone who hurt you continue to live in your mind? Your thoughts are yours don't hand them over to someone who didn't value your heart. If you are struggling with a burden, ask yourself this:

- Do you have a problem?
- If no: Then why worry?
- If yes: Can you do something about it?
- If yes: Take action and stop worrying.
- If no: Since you can't change it, why worry?

Reflect and Realign

Take a moment to turn your pain into a lesson.

The Note to Self:

Take a piece of paper and divide it into two columns.

1. In the first column, Blame them: List the sleep you lost, the tears you cried, and the way you felt. Acknowledge the hurt.
2. In the second column, Bless them: List the lessons you learned, the strength you gained, and the clarity you now have about who you don't want to become.

You can either stay bitter about the past or be better because of it. The choice is always yours.

Let it hurt. Let it teach you. Then let it go.

❋❋❋

Chapter - 3

Going Inward: The Practice That Changed Everything

"When you quiet the outside world, the inside starts speaking the truth."

We live in a world that constantly screams for our attention social media notifications, city noise, social pressure, and the endless hustle. For a long time, I was trapped in that loop. I was distracted, anxious, and constantly trying to "fix" my life from the outside while completely ignoring the engine room within.

I didn't start meditating because I was calm. I started because I was breaking.

Finding the Pause

There was a time when I felt completely scattered. I was showing up everywhere for college, for friends, for events but I wasn't showing up for myself. I was living entirely in my head, overthinking every decision and comparing my path to everyone else's. I would scroll through Instagram and feel "behind" in life. I would smile in public but feel a deep, hollow anxiety the moment I was alone.

I discovered a practice I now call the 6-Phase Meditation. I didn't expect a miracle; I just needed a pause. The first day felt awkward. By the third day, I found myself in tears. They weren't tears of sadness, but of relief. For the first time in years, I was finally listening to my own voice.

From Awareness to Action: The Silent Worker

As I deepened my practice, specifically through my morning grounding and chanting my Kuldev mantra (Om Shree Mallikarjunay Namahah), my understanding of the world changed. When you go inward, you start seeing outward—not with judgment, but with genuine gratitude.

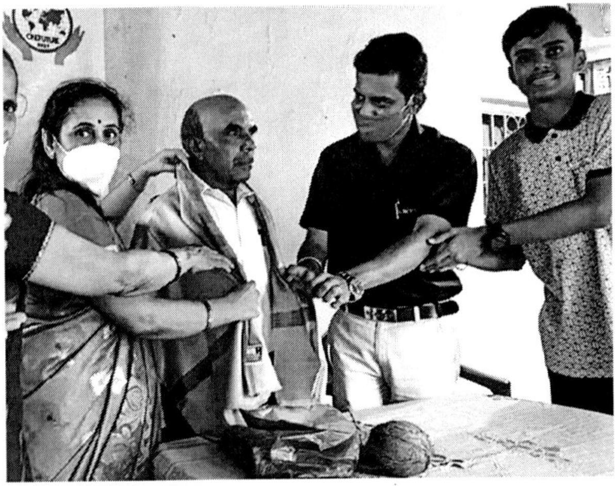

In the 11th standard, through an initiative called Salute the Silent Worker, I began to notice a postman who passed our home every day. He was a sincere, humble man, always wearing a smile despite being close to retirement. Because my internal "noise" had quieted, I could truly see his dedication. We organized a small program to honor him. I wrote a poem for him, and we invited his family.

Seeing that man falling into tears ,a silent worker finally feel seen and recognized was a lesson no textbook could teach. It confirmed that the more we connect with ourselves, the more we can connect with the "unsung heroes" of humanity. A moment decades in the making

The 6-Phase Toolkit

This isn't about emptying your mind; it's about intentionally designing your emotional state.

Phase 1: Compassion & Kindness

Visualize yourself radiating kindness. Imagine feeding a stray dog or helping a stranger. This shifts your identity from a "critic" to a "connector."

Phase 2: Gratitude

Acknowledge beauty even in the midst of pain. Gratitude is the single strongest trait linked to human well-being. Think of your parents, your health, and even the challenges that forced you to grow.

Phase 3: Forgiveness

Release the poison. Say it clearly: "I release this burden. I no longer carry it." This makes space for healing and stops you from living in the past.

Phase 4: Vision for Life

Dream boldly. Whether it's inspiring thousands on a stage or running a business, see it and feel it. Your vision becomes your direction.

Phase 5: Action Today (The 1% Rule)

A dream without action is a fantasy. What is the smallest step you can take today? Growth compounds; your future is built from your "todays."

Phase 6: Feeling Supported

This is the most emotional phase. Imagine yourself supported by your parents, your ancestors, or the universe. Know that you are not alone; you are being guided and cared for.

Reflect and Realign

Meditation isn't magic, but it unlocks the magic within you. You cannot always control the thoughts that pop into your head, but through these phases, you choose which ones you give power to.

Your Challenge:

Try this 6-phase process for just 15 minutes a day for the next 21 days. I promise you, the person who finishes those three weeks will not be the same person who started them.

Meditation Isn't Magic, It's Muscle

As a physiotherapist, I spend my days helping

people restore movement and strengthen their bodies. I know that if a patient wants to walk again after an injury, they don't just wish for it—they do the reps. They put in the work, one small movement at a time, to rebuild the connection between their brain and their muscles.

I've come to realize that the mind works the same way.

You don't need to be a saint or a monk to practice the 6-Phase Meditation. You just need to treat it like physical therapy for your soul. Visualization, when practiced daily, isn't "magic"—it is a form of cognitive conditioning. It reshapes your neural pathways, and just as physical exercise reshapes your body, these mental "reps" reshape your life.

Think of this practice as your Personal GPS. Life will always have traffic, roadblocks, and unexpected turns. But when you have a daily grounding practice, you have a compass that leads you back to inner peace, ensures you make an outer impact, and keeps you connected to who you truly are

***

Chapter - 4

The Power Behind My Beads

My journey with chanting didn't start at a temple or in a high-profile spiritual seminar. It began in my own neighborhood when I was just a boy in the eighth standard.

There is a lady we all lovingly call Chachi. She has been my mentor since I was three years old a neighbor who became family in spirit. It was Chachi who first handed me a mala and gently showed me how to chant with it. That simple, quiet moment was where it all began. From there, my relationship with mantras evolved from a simple habit to a form of healing, and eventually, to something sacred.

The Pulse of the Mahakumbh

While Chachi gave me the tool, it was the Mahakumbh that revealed its true power. There is no place on earth quite like it a sea of humanity gathered at the banks of the Triveni Sangam, where the Ganga, Yamuna, and the mythical Saraswati meet. The air there doesn't just carry sound; it carries a weight, a collective vibration of millions of souls seeking something higher.

As I stood at the water's edge, surrounded by the scent of incense and the distant roar of thousands of devotees, I closed my eyes. The world outside vanished. I began to softly breathe out: Om Namah Shivaya.

In that moment, I didn't just recite words; I felt a deep wave of peace and energy surge through me, as if the divine had touched my soul. It was then I truly understood that a mantra is not just a word; it is a frequency that reorganizes the self from the inside out.

The Physics of Intention

What truly amplifies a mantra or any affirmation is the intention behind it. I've discovered that these "mental reps" work best when three elements collide:

1. Concise positive words
2. Clear visualization
3. Genuine emotion

Nikola Tesla once said: "If you want to find the secrets of the universe, think in terms of energy, frequency, and vibration." Everything our thoughts, feelings, and actions is energy. If you hold a thought with clarity and emotion long enough, it becomes your reality. That's not philosophy; it's physics.

We don't attract what we want. We attract what we are.

The Daily Reset

Chanting is not just repetition; it is alignment. When I repeat, "I am strong. I am evolving. I am guided," I do it with feeling. I close my eyes and visualize the strength moving through me.

These chants are reminders that who I become is the result of what I think, feel, and believe repeated over time. When my mind is cluttered, I return to my beads to raise my frequency.

A New Chapter Unfolds

As I walked away from the Mahakumbh, carrying the echo of mantras and a weightless strength of faith, I thought I had discovered enough to last a lifetime.

But life has a way of reminding us that the journey never truly ends. Sometimes the next step doesn't arrive as a grand pilgrimage or a sacred river. Sometimes, it arrives as something small and forgotten, lying in the corner of your own room a diary.

Little did I know that flipping through its pages would feel like meeting my younger self again, and that the boy I once was had already planted the seeds for the man I was becoming.

At the banks of the Triveni Sangam during the Mahakumbh. In this moment, the noise of millions faded into a single vibration. Offering water to the river wasn't just a ritual; it was a physical act of letting go of the old self to make room for the light.

It was here I realized that when you align your frequency with the Divine, the world outside finally begins to make sense.

***

Chapter - 5

Seeds from My Diary

It was one of those lazy afternoons when the house was quiet, the air still, and the sunlight fell slant through the window. I was searching for something an old paper, maybe a misplaced bill when my hand brushed against a small diary. The cover was faded, the corners worn, but the moment I saw the years embossed on it 2019, 2021 a wave of memories came rushing back.

I opened it casually at first, not expecting much. But as the pages turned, I realized I was staring into the mind of my younger self. Each page carried not just ink, but a hunger the search of a boy looking for meaning, direction, and a way to be happy.

The Blueprint of Balance

On the very first page, my eyes caught a line: "Keep your mind self-centered around yourself and keep your heart centered around others."

I paused. At seventeen, what did I truly know about balance? Back then, I must have scribbled it after watching a video or reading a random article. Yet now, years later, those words hit me with the weight of lived experience. How many times had I let my mind wander outward, chasing validation, and lost my peace? And how many times had I closed my heart when it was needed most? That one line was a blueprint a message from the boy I was to the man I was becoming.

Happiness in the Small Corners

Further in, another line made me smile: "Spend time with kids and animals (getting a lot of happiness)."

It was so simple, almost innocent. But as I read it, I remembered the joy of playing with a neighborhood dog and the way a child's laughter could erase the weight of a hard day. It struck me: happiness had always been hiding in the small corners of life. I had written it down then, and life had been reminding me ever since.

The Helper's High

The next entry had a bold title: Helper's High.

"The time when you give someone something, the feeling is helper's high, even when we initiate a positive conversation." Behind the youthful phrasing was a truth I have now lived many times. That lightness after helping a stranger, the glow of a kind conversation, the way energy shifts when you give without expecting anything in return that was already hidden in those few words.

Under-Commit, Over-Deliver

As I turned more pages, one line stood out with sharp clarity: "Under-commitment, over-delivery here result comes. It doesn't grow multiple, but it grows exponentially."

At nineteen, I barely understood exponential growth. But today, I realize how true it is. Whether in my studies, my community service, or public speaking, the times I quietly worked and gave more than I promised were the times life rewarded me in ways beyond calculation. My diary had unknowingly recorded a success principle I now carry in my heart.

The Mental Garden

But the entry that touched me most was this one: "Our mind is a garden and we are beautiful flowers. Negative thoughts are like weeds; throw them out or they will suck the nutrition of your mind."

I closed my eyes and let that sink in. In 2021, I had written it as a metaphor. Today, I live it. Every morning, when I sit with my beads, when I chant, and when I repeat my affirmations, I am doing exactly what that page told me: pulling out the weeds and watering the flowers.

Conclusion: The Message for You

That day, I didn't just read a diary. I met myself. I realized that wisdom doesn't always come from the outside. Sometimes, it is already written within us waiting for us to live a little longer, to stumble, to rise, and then to finally understand.

Your younger self may already hold the wisdom your older self will one day need. Imagine if, every day, you wrote down just one good thing that happened to you. By the end of the year, you would have 365 moments of joy to look back on. That, too, is how we plant seeds. That, too, is how gardens grow.

The Challenge:

Write, reflect, and return to your own words. Start writing one thing which happens in that particular day. Start keeping count of the blessings you once overlooked. You might find that the universe has been speaking to you all along you just had to learn its language.

Chapter - 6

The Real You

There are moments in life incidences that strike without warning that force you to stop and look at yourself in a way you never have before. I won't deny the fact that I recently walked through one such moment myself on (7/2/2026). It was a period that stripped away my comfort and left me standing face-to-face with a question I thought I had already answered: Who am I, really?

"YOU VS YOU"

They say the trees at the Hadimba Devi Temple in Manali have seen a thousand seekers, each carrying a heavy bag of labels. On 7/2/2026, I set mine down at the forest's edge. This isn't a picture of a traveler; it's a picture of a student learning to stand

still. I realized that if I can't be happy as 'nothing' under these trees, I will never be truly happy as 'everything' on a stage. The ultimate competition has always been YOU VS YOU.

Beyond the Social Tags

If you were to introduce yourself to me right now, what would you say? Most of us reach for our social tags immediately. We mention our occupation, our nationality, our ethnicity, or where we grew up. We talk about our religion or our hobbies as if they are the boundaries of our being.

But these are superficial markers—labels we use to categorize ourselves so society knows where to "place" us. Most people spend their entire lives building these labels rather than building an identity. They become their job title; they become their achievements; they become their origin story.

But what happens when the titles fade? When no one cares what you do or where you are from? What is left when the world stops validating your roles?

The Essence and the Soul

Stripping away these markers forces us to think about our essence. Your true self isn't your name, your job, or your background it is your values, your energy, and your presence.

The world will always try to define you by your roles, but your soul can only be defined by your purpose. Real success isn't about the exhausting race to become someone important in the eyes of others. It is about the quiet, radical act of remembering who you already are.

Through my recent struggle, my perspective shifted. I stopped looking at people through the lens of their social tags. Now, I am able to see and hear you for your essence and your soul. I see your worth without needing to see your trophies. I feel your groundedness without needing to hear your recognition.

Learning to Stand Still

Meeting yourself beyond your achievements is perhaps the hardest work you will ever do. It requires you to be okay with being "nothing" by the world's standards so that you can be "everything" by your own.

It is easy to be confident when you are winning. It is much harder and much more honest to feel your worth when you are simply sitting in a quiet room, with no medals to show and no one to impress. But that is where the "Real You" lives. In the silence. In the values you hold when no one is watching. In the energy you bring to a room before you even speak a word.

❋❋❋

Chapter - 7

The Bond Beyond Time (Family members)

Whatever good thing I do, the first people I want to share it with are my grandparents and also parents It doesn't matter if it is something big, like winning a competition, or something small, like helping a stranger on the street for me, every small moment of pride, every act of kindness, every step of growth belongs to them too.

And the best part is, they receive it with the same joy, sometimes even more than I feel myself. Their eyes light up, their smiles widen, and suddenly, that small moment becomes a festival at home. To them, nothing is ordinary when it comes to their grandchildren.

I remember one moment very clearly during one of the competition Student of the Year in College. In that competition, I was asked about my role model. Without hesitation, I said, "My grandfather." Later, when I told him, I saw a kind of happiness on his face that words can't capture. His eyes sparkled, his chest swelled with pride, and for a second, he looked both surprised and deeply moved. That joy that silent, overflowing joy was unmatchable. No award, no applause, no recognition from the outside world has ever felt as pure as that moment did for me.

This is why I feel it's important to write about them in this book. Because this bond is something beyond words, beyond logic, beyond explanation. It is the kind of love that touches the ground root of who I am. As an Indian kid, as a small-town boy, this bond matters more than anything else.

My grandparents never asked me for medals or certificates. What they wanted was much simpler, much deeper: to see me live with kindness, to see me stand with courage, to see me grow without forgetting where I came from. And every time I achieved something, no matter how small, I knew it wasn't just my success. It was theirs too.

My soil and my soul. Sitting here on these steps, I realize I am only the tree; they are the roots. Every blossom I carry is a result of the lifetime they spent watering the ground beneath my feet.

Roots and wings

Beyond the celebrations and the shared pride, there is a deeper gift they gave me: the comfort of silence. With the rest of the world, I often feel the pressure to talk, to explain, or to perform. But with them, I can simply be. Sitting on the porch or sharing a simple meal, no words are needed to prove my worth. In their presence, my "essence"—the real me—is enough. They are the only people who don't need me to be "someone" because, to them, I have always been everything.

When I look back, I realize that this bond is not just about me and my grandparents. It is about the invisible thread that ties generations together. They gave me roots so I could grow wings. They showed me that family isn't a support system you lean on only in tough times it is the soil from which your strength grows every single day.

Today, when I share my story, I want every reader to remember , but the moments you share with family who live for your smile those are the treasures that never fade.

Celebrate your small victories with your family, because in their joy you'll discover the true value of your journey.

Reflect and Realign: The Roots Challenge

Take a piece of paper and write down one small thing you achieved recently something you are proud of that you haven't shared with your "roots" yet. Then, make the call. Share the joy.

Chapter - 8

The Art of Showing Up

There is a specific kind of silence that happens when your life feels like a mess. It's the sound of the world rushing past you while you feel anchored to a single, difficult spot. In those moments, the weight of your own thoughts can feel heavy enough to break you.

We are taught that progress must be visible that if we aren't "fixing" things or "understanding" the reasons behind our pain, we are failing. But there is a deeper truth in the stillness.

The Speed Breaker

On February 7th, 2026, I hit a speed breaker that I didn't see coming. In the world of medical studies, we are taught to be perfect, but that day, the results said otherwise

For a moment, everything stopped. I felt a deep sense of shame. I didn't want to show up at college. I didn't want to see my friends. I wanted to hide.

But here is the truth about speed breakers: They are not walls. A wall stops you; a speed breaker just asks you to slow down, reassess your gear, and then move forward again with more caution.

Looking at this boy, I see a heart full of unshielded hope. He didn't know about the 'speed breakers', but his dreams are the reason I refuse to stay down. To find the strength to move forward, I had to go back to these roots and find the version of myself that hadn't yet learned how to doubt. I'm not just showing up for my future; I'm showing up to make this little version of me proud of the man he is becoming. I owe it to him, and to the two people standing beside him, to never stop halfway. I had to go back, to find the real me.

If your life is a mess right now, just don't quit. If your thoughts feel heavy, stick with it. If you feel stuck while everyone else is moving, keep showing up.

Stop trying to fix everything tonight. Stop trying to understand every "why" right now. Showing up when it's hard builds you; it makes you wiser and stronger. It helps you learn from what hurt you.

We often look for grand closures or cinematic breakthroughs. We want the wound to vanish instantly. But time has a different rhythm. The days you are just trying to get through "today" are the very days you will be most proud of tomorrow.

They are the days where the real work happens the invisible healing of the wounds you don't even talk about. Survival isn't always a roar. Sometimes, it's just the quiet decision to show up again.

❋❋❋

Chapter - 9

The Divine Detour: Mahakumbh

Sometimes, the most profound journeys begin with a simple, hesitant "yes."

It started on an ordinary day when my classmate Nitish, a true travel enthusiast, threw an idea into the air: "Let's go to Mahakumbh."

My immediate reaction was the voice of logic. My mind the same mind that used to over-analyze everything started listing the hurdles. What about college attendance? How will I get leave? The trains will be packed. It's too short notice. We had no tickets, no itinerary, and no return plan. To a logical mind, it was a recipe for disaster.

But Nitish didn't operate on fear; he operated on faith. That very night, he figured out a special train, booked the tickets, and said, "We leave tomorrow."

I looked at the tickets, then at my parents. With their blessing and a sudden surge of adrenaline, we packed a bag of eatables and boarded the train. We didn't know how we would return; we only knew we had to go.

The 36-Hour Pilgrim

The journey was a grueling 36 hours, but something shifted in that carriage. We met strangers who weren't just travelers; they were seekers. We shared food and stories with people whose eyes held a different kind of spark a spiritual fire. The conversation wasn't about politics or the economy; it was about the soul. The train ride itself became a preparation, tuning my frequency from "student" to "pilgrim."

The River of Humanity

When we arrived, the scale of it hit me. "Crowd" is too small a word. It was a sea of humanity crores of people flowing like a river toward the Sangam. We stayed with some senior relatives, witnessing the raw reality of the city including the intense struggle of UPSC aspirants living in small rooms, fighting for their future. It was a humbling backdrop to the spiritual grandeur.

The next day, we moved toward the Triveni Sangam. The energy was so magnetic that the laws of physics seemed to suspend. We walked and walked. Later, we calculated that we had walked nearly 40 kilometers that day. Under normal circumstances, my legs would have given up. But there, amidst the chanting, the incense, and the collective faith of millions, I didn't feel a thing. I was being carried by a force larger than my own muscles.

The Dip and The Light

Reaching the Triveni Sangam—the confluence of three rivers—was a moment I cannot fully translate into language. Stepping into that water wasn't just a bath; it was a reset. As I took the holy dip, surrounded by the chants of the Akharas and the vibration of bells, the "social tags" I wrote about earlier dissolved into the water.

That night, witnessing the Triveni Sangam Aarti was an out-of-body experience. The lamps mirrored the stars, and the chanting synced with my heartbeat. The vibe was distinct ancient yet immediate. I wasn't just watching a ritual; I was witnessing the heartbeat of the universe.

The Kashi Test

The journey didn't end there. We moved on to Varanasi (Kashi), traversing the Ghats by boat and navigating the narrow, winding gullies to reach Kashi Vishwanath. But, as with all pilgrimages, there were hurdles. Our bus broke down in the middle of nowhere.

In the past, I would have panicked. I would have cursed the lack of planning. But this time, I smiled. I realized that the breakdown wasn't an error; it was a pause. It gave us a moment to breathe before the intensity of Kashi. We finally made it. Witnessing the Ganga Aarti live was the crescendo a symphony of fire and water that silenced the noise of the mind completely.

No picture can capture what it feels like to stand here. When the Ganga Aarti begins, time just stops. Surrounded by the chanting of mantras and the warmth of the holy fire, my mind went completely silent. It was the most beautiful, overwhelming moment of my life. I just stood there in the crowd with folded hands and tears in my eyes, completely at peace.

The Capital Bonus

The magic didn't even stop when we left the holy cities. Our return journey took us through

Delhi, where we had a 12-hour layover before the Rajdhani Express arrived. Still buzzing with the energy of the trip, we decided to visit the Red Fort.

There was a quiz competition happening for students my Central Ministry. On a whim just like the rest of this trip we participated. And in that flow state, without any preparation, Nitish and I both won the title of "Best Participant."

It was proof that when you are spiritually aligned and open to the unknown, you don't just survive the journey; you thrive in it. Whether it was the holy water of the Sangam or a history stage in the capital, the "unplanned self" was winning everywhere.

The Lesson: The Planned Unplanned

The only message I want to leave you with in this chapter is this: Sometimes, your unplanned self creates the best travel.

We spend so much of our lives trying to micromanage every minute, terrified of the unknown. But this trip taught me that when the motive is pure when the destination is spiritual you don't need a map. God has already decided the route for you.

We had no return ticket, but we returned richer than we left. We had no hotel bookings, but we found shelter. We had no plan, but we found purpose.

Allow life to give you opportunities that don't fit into your calendar. Say yes to the chaos. Pack your bag without knowing the return date. Because it is often in the detour that we finally meet our destiny.

Reflection

Is there a "Nitish" in your life inviting you on an adventure you are too afraid to take? Trust the unplanned.

❋❋❋

Chapter - 10

ISKCON Lessons: Decoding the Gita

Hare Krishna, Hare Krishna,
Krishna Krishna, Hare Hare

Hare Rama, Hare Rama,
Rama Rama, Hare Hare

For the last four years, I have been associated with ISKCON, having deep conversations with monks about the wisdom of the Bhagavad Gita. Since childhood, I was raised in the culture of Sanatana Dharma, but there is a difference between following a ritual and understanding the truth.

All our scriptures, at their core, teach us one fundamental reality: Change is constant.

When Lord Krishna speaks to Arjuna in the Gita, the first thing He emphasizes is the temporary nature of this world. Today there is happiness; tomorrow there may be distress. Today there is praise; tomorrow there may be criticism. Today there is success; tomorrow there may be failure.

The World of Duality

We live in a world of duality. Light and dark, hot and cold, joy and sorrow. The problem isn't that these changes happen; the problem is that we get shocked when they do. We live with the illusion that good times should last forever.

So, what is the solution? Krishna gives one word: Tolerance.

But tolerance doesn't mean being weak. It means knowing that no situation is permanent. We should not become complacent and arrogant when we are winning, nor should we become depressed and broken when we are losing. To maintain this balance, we need Inner Strength. And I have realized that Inner Strength is synonymous with Spiritual Strength.

Sweat in Peace, Bleed Less in War

There is a saying my college professor once shared that stuck with me forever. It is an old Army saying

"Those who sweat in peace, bleed less in war."

In Hindi, we have a similar doha:

"Dukh mein sumiran sab kare,
sukh mein kare na koi.
Jo sukh mein sumiran kare,
toh dukh kaahe ko hoi."

(Everyone remembers God in times of sorrow, but no one remembers Him in joy. If you remembered Him during your joy, the sorrow would not touch you.)

Many people treat God like an emergency room—they only go when there is a trauma. But spirituality is not a cure for a crisis; it is the immunity against it.

When you do your Sadhana (practice) and your chanting during the good times (peace), you are building armor. This doesn't mean you won't face difficulties. A spiritual person still faces failures and "topsy-turvy" moments. But the difference is this: The failure will not be able to break you.

The Speed Breaker Analogy

Human life is special because God has given us a superpower: Free Will. The ability to choose our response.

Imagine you are driving down a road and you hit a massive, unexpected speed breaker. You have two choices:

Choice 1: Lamentation (The "Why Me?" Mode)

You can stop the car, get out, and curse the person who built the speed breaker. You can blame the government. You can scream, "Why did God let this happen to me?"

Result: You are stuck. You are angry. And the speed breaker is still there.

Choice 2: Anticipation and Action

You realize the car took a hit. You check for damage. If it's broken, you take it to the garage. You repair it. Then, you get back in, press the accelerator, and move ahead.

Result: You continue your journey.

Life is full of speed breakers. Complaining has never solved a single issue in the history of humanity. The only thing that works is Acceptance and Anticipation. Accept that the road is bumpy, prepare your vehicle (your mind) in advance, and when the hit comes, handle it and keep moving.

Sharanagati: The Ultimate Safety Net

People often ask, "When these massive changes come, what do we do?" The answer the scriptures give is Sharanagati—Surrender.

This isn't giving up. It is the confidence that God has said, "Anyone who reaches out to Me will never be let down." We must make ourselves so internally strong that the external duality cannot shake us.

Human life is precious. The number of breaths you will take is fixed. You don't have time to stay stuck at the speed breaker. Stop asking "Why me?" and start saying "Try me."

Sometimes we win, and sometimes we learn. But with God as the anchor, we never stop moving.

The Purpose: Why Do We Exist?

But why are we on this road in the first place?

I remember a story where a monk asked his teacher, Srila Prabhupada, "What is the purpose of life?"

Prabhupada answered simply: "To enjoy."

At first, this sounds surprising. Isn't spirituality about Strictness? But he wasn't talking about cheap, temporary enjoyment. The scriptures use the phrase / Ananda-mayo 'bhyasat /the very nature of the soul is to seek happiness.

We are not designed to be miserable. If we want to find the deepest type of happiness, we need to get the deepest sense of our own identity. In the Bhagavad Gita, Krishna explains that every soul is unique. You are not a photocopy. You have unique abilities and a unique journey. While spiritual truths are universal, your path back to them is individual.

The Anxiety Antidote

One of the most valuable lessons in the Gita addresses the biggest epidemic of our generation:

Anxiety, Nervousness, and Depression.

Why is it so difficult for us to handle pressure? Why do we crumble before an exam or an interview?

Because we are attached to the results. We want the trophy before we run the race.

The most peace-giving verse in the Gita answers this:

Karmanye vadhikaraste ma phaleshu kadachana

"(You have a right to perform your prescribed duty, but you are not entitled to the fruits of action.)"

Krishna is saying: Focus on the effort. The result is not in your hands.

This brings me to a line I want you to write on your heart:

"The pain of discipline is uncomfortable, but the pain of regret is unbearable." - Said by one of the monk of ISCKON

The 5 Factors of Success

We shouldn't worry about results—but that doesn't mean we become lazy. It means we give 100%

effort. If the result is bad, we accept it and move on. If the result is good, we don't get arrogant.

According to the Gita, the result of any action depends on 5 factors. We usually think "I did it," but we are just one part of the equation:

1. The Doer (Karta): The person doing the act.
2. The Place (Adhisthanam): The field or body where it is done.
3. The Instruments (Karanam): Our senses and mind.
4. The Effort (Chesta): The hard work we put in.
5. Destiny (Daivam): The sanction of the divine.

Sometimes, you have the first four perfect. You studied hard, you showed up, you did the work. But the fifth factor—Destiny—says "No."

This is where most people break. They think they failed. But if you understand this science, you realize you didn't fail; the fifth factor just wasn't aligned yet.

The Override: The God Guarantee

But is there a way to influence that fifth factor? Yes.

There is one force even greater than Destiny. When we pay attention to this, our restlessness turns into peace. That factor is God's Grace.

In the last shlok of the Gita, Krishna gives the ultimate password:

Sarva-dharman parityajya mam
ekam sharanam vraja

"(Abandon all varieties of religion and just surrender unto Me.)"

And He gives a guarantee: Ma shuchah—"Do not fear." He promises, "I will deliver you from all sinful reactions."

There is a powerful Sanskrit line: Karmapi nirdughati kintu cha bhakti bhajanam. It means that while Karma is strong, Bhakti (Devotion) can burn Karma.

In this age of Kali Yuga, the most potent way to access this grace is through Chanting. It is the best technique because it has no hard rules. You can chant while sitting, while walking to class, while working, or at any time. Chanting connects you to the source, and when you are connected to the source, destiny can be rewritten.

A Request to the Reader

Someone once told me a beautiful thing: "We have to learn to see the world through the eyes of scriptures."

My purpose in writing this chapter is small. If even a few of my readers start following this if you start

"sweating in peace" then my purpose is fulfilled.

God says in the Gita that the person who shares this wisdom with others is His favorite. So, take this wisdom. Use it. Share it with your friends and family who aren't aware of it.

Watch how your life changes from "Why me?" to "Grace is with me."

This picture of my Janmashtami service at ISKCON is a living reminder of Krishna's core message in the Gita. True happiness is found the moment you stop working for your own ego and start serving with pure devotion. When you offer your efforts to God, life stops being a battlefield and becomes a blessing.

❋❋❋

Chapter - 11

Connecting the Dots

The year did not begin with perfect clarity. In fact, it started with a familiar rhythm of heavy ups and downs. I was still navigating the emotional hangover of my academic "speed breaker," trying to keep my mindset positive when I was, quite frankly, figuring absolutely nothing out.

Sometimes, when your mind is a tangled mess, the universe decides to physically move you. For me, that movement started with a South Zone chess championship that pulled me down to Tamil Nadu.

I found myself exploring the extreme South of India. I walked through the ancient, vibrant streets of Madurai and Thanjavur. I stood in absolute awe before the Sri Ranganathaswamy Temple the largest functioning Hindu temple in the world. There is a specific kind of grounding you feel when you stand in front of architecture that has survived centuries; it silently reminds you that your current problems are incredibly small in the grand timeline of the world.

But while I was soaking in the spiritual heat of the South, my phone was buzzing with a completely different energy. My childhood friends back home were relentlessly plotting a trip to North India specifically Delhi and the mountains of Himachal Pradesh.

They were practically dragging me into the plan. Logistically, it was a nightmare. Connecting the dots from the deep corners of Tamil Nadu all the way up to the freezing altitudes of Himachal seemed like too much friction for a mind that was already tired. My default habit of overthinking kicked in. Should I go? Is it too much travel? What about my schedule?

But if there is one thing I have learned on this journey, it is that sometimes you have to tell your logical brain to shut up. I booked a flight from Chennai to Delhi.

Landing in Delhi and reuniting with my childhood friends was like breathing fresh air after being underwater. There is a magic to day-one friends. They do not care about your medical degree, your academic failures, or the "social tags" you carry. They just know you. They are the same guys who will relentlessly make fun of you, roast your life choices, and then physically carry your bags when you are exhausted.

From Delhi, we pushed North, leaving the plains behind and entering the immense, quiet power of Himachal Pradesh. We hit Manali, Kullu, and the winding roads of the high altitudes.

I realized something profound as we climbed higher into the Himalayas: You either love the mountains, or you haven't visited them yet. Life in the mountains operates on a different frequency. Witnessing my first real snowfall, standing surrounded by the towering, silent peaks it strips you of your ego. The mountains do not care about your stress. They just exist, massive and beautiful, demanding nothing but your presence.

For 15 days, we were constantly on the move. It was an absolute crash course in living. We faced hurdles, unexpected delays, freezing temperatures, and situations completely out of our control. But when you are with your brothers, a broken-down plan just becomes a hilarious memory. We navigated the chaos together, laughing through the discomfort, fueled by the sheer adrenaline of being young and free.

This 15-day journey from the ancient temples of the South to the snow-capped peaks of the North transformed something deep inside me. It showed me the staggering diversity, culture, and beauty of our own country. India has an entire universe to offer within its borders.

Every guy in his twenties should travel to know himself, because the comfort zone is a beautiful place, but nothing ever grows there. When you are sitting in your room, grinding through your daily routine, you are defined by your syllabus, your career anxieties, and the heavy expectations of everyone around you.

But when you are freezing on a mountain in Himachal, or trying to navigate a broken itinerary at 2 AM with your brothers, all those “social tags” completely vanish. The road strips you down to your absolute core. The mountains do not care about the exams you passed or the subjects you failed. The journey forces you to meet the real you the guy who has to be patient when things go wrong, the guy who has to find humor in a crisis, and the guy who finally realizes that the world is far too massive to spend a lifetime stressing over a single bad day.

❄❄❄

Chapter - 12

Dare to Dream

There is a famous saying that has echoed through the corridors of our schools and the pages of countless books, yet we rarely stop to actually understand its weight: A dream is not what you see in your sleep; a dream is that which does not let you sleep. It is a profound truth. A real dream doesn't happen when your eyes are closed and your mind is resting. A real dream stays with you all day. It sits in the back of your mind while you are sitting in a lecture, walking down the street, or eating your lunch.

But to find that dream, you have to be intentional. Nothing changes in our life until we change, and change is the most constant thing in the universe.

If you can invest a little time in your life asking yourself the important questions Who do I want to be? How do I want to live my life? What do I really want? everything shifts. Instead of turning on your cell phone and getting distracted by the noise of the world, discipline yourself. Take an hour just to answer these questions. Write them down. Review them. Get very clear on your vision.

When I look back at my own journey, I realize that everything I am today started with one of those clear visions. I was in the 7th standard . Like any other school day, we were gathered for an event, and a chief guest walked onto the stage. He was a public speaker, dressed sharply in a crisp suit and polished boots. If you want to grow, you have to think of the people you admire and start making different choices to emulate their best qualities. For me, that speaker was the blueprint. I sat there in the audience, a young kid in a school uniform, and a thought planted itself in my head: I want to do that. I want to wear a suit and boots and speak on that stage.

It was a small seed, but I refused to let it go. By the time I entered the Ninth standard, I started executing. I stepped onto the school stage. From the school level, I pushed to the state level. And then, the dream that started in a seventh-standard auditorium took me across borders to represent our nation at the JCI Public Speaking Championship in Thailand. Somewhere along the way, you just have to trust the unknown and take the leap.

A young kid in a school uniform sat in an auditorium, saw a man in a crisp suit, and made a silent decision: 'I want to do that.' From that public speaking championship winner. This isn't just a picture of me in a suit; it is the visual proof that once you decide you want a good life, the universe begins to align.

Through this journey, I have learned a fundamental rule about the universe: Once you decide you want to have a good life, life will actually start getting good. We might not realize it, but a lot of us are walking around undecided, carrying a negative attitude towards life, the people around us, and the things that have happened to us. When we walk around undecided and harbor this negativity, that is exactly what we attract. But when you finally decide that you want to have a good life, things start to change. Things start to align. You are here on this earth, so you might as well decide that life is going to be good.

You should try to see how far you can go. See what you can do in this life, because the saddest thing I see isn't people who try and fail; it is people who simply do not dream at all.

Dreams do not always have to be about standing on international stages or building massive empires. The beauty of dreaming lies in its simplicity. It can be as simple as saying: I want to travel. I want to write. I want to study and master this subject. I want to start a small business. I want to groom myself well. I want to marry a specific type of girl who understands my soul. I want to buy that particular bike and take it on a ride. I want to own a beautiful car. These simple, deeply personal dreams act as your anchor. The world is full of possibilities, and there are so many cool places you can go and see. You don't need to have it all figured out on day one. You just need your hands, a dream in your heart, and some courage, and you go.

Your life is a blank page, and your dreams are the ink. Pick up the pen, write your story, and never, ever go back to sleep.

❋❋❋

God Calling

Just days before sending this book to print when I thought every lesson had been learned and every story closed my phone rang. It was my friend, Bobby. Out of nowhere, he pitched a spontaneous spiritual journey across Hyderabad and Andhra Pradesh.

Usually, my mind would weigh the logistics, the timing, and the exhaustion of traveling right before a major milestone. But this time, I didn't hesitate for a single second. When the divine invites you, you simply say yes.

Our route began at Kurnool Junction AP, leading us straight into the winding, breathtaking ghats of the Nallamala Hills. The drive toward Srisailam was spectacular; the dense hills and ancient roads didn't just transport us physically, they prepared us mentally. By the time we reached the sacred grounds of the Mallikarjuna Jyotirlinga, a profound quiet had settled over me.

At the entrance, I made a silent decision. From my very first step at the gates all the way into the deepest part of the main temple entrance, I continuously chanted: Om Sri Mallikarjuna Namaha.

With every step and every chant, the energy inside the temple became absolutely overwhelming. It was the exact same pure, fabulous vibration I had experienced on the ghats of Kashi. Standing there in Dakshina Kashi, I realized that while geography changes, the frequency of the divine remains absolute.

After seeking the blessings of Sakshi Ganapati the divine witness to our pilgrimage we traveled onward to the magnificent Swarnagiri Sri Venkateswara Swamy Temple. The view that unfolded before my eyes was straight out of a divine dream. I stood looking over the temple's grand, intricately carved stone courtyard. In the very center lay a serene, sacred water pool, and resting peacefully amidst the water was a magnificent dark stone idol of the Lord reclining gracefully on the multi-hooded serpent. As the soft, warm glow of the evening lights illuminated the endless rows of pillars, the towering gopurams, and the grand Namam gracing the main entrance, a wave of pure emotion washed over me. Looking at that serene scene, surrounded by such devoted craftsmanship and the quiet presence of other seekers, the entire fast-paced world outside those walls seemed to simply pause.

This wasn't just a random trip with a friend; . God was calling.

Standing there, the ultimate truth finally clicked. We can chase every ambition, write every book, and climb every mountain, but the deepest peace you will ever feel is when you drop your ego, bow your head, and realize you were never walking alone. We spend so much of our youth trying to control every single outcome, forgetting that there is a higher power gently guiding our steps. He gives us the strength to keep running, but more importantly, He gives us the grace to stand still and just breathe.

If there is a message I can leave you with from this quiet, sacred place, it is this: give your absolute best to your dreams, but never let the rush of life steal your inner peace. When the world feels too loud, and the pressure of the future gets too heavy, close your eyes and surrender it to the divine. You don't have to carry the weight of the world all by yourself. Work hard, take responsibility for your journey, but always trust the detours. Keep your faith unshaken, and know that while the effort is entirely up to you, the universe has already written a beautiful destination for your soul.

❋❋❋

Epilogue

The Quiet Morning After

As I sit down to write these final words, there is a profound stillness. The stages have been swept, the Himalayan cold has faded from my jacket, and the chanting crowds of the Mahakumbh are now a beautiful memory. I am back to the reality of my everyday life the heavy textbooks, the quiet evenings, the daily routine.

There is a temptation, when you write a book, to sound like you have crossed the final finish line. To sound like you have decoded the universe and will never struggle again.

But I want to leave you with the absolute, unfiltered truth. I am twenty-two years old, and I haven't figured it all out.

Tomorrow morning, my alarm will ring, and I will have to choose to show up all over again. I will still face days where my mind feels heavy. I will still encounter speed breakers that I didn't see coming. I will still have moments of doubt, exams that test my patience, and days where the road feels a little too long.

I didn't write this book because I am perfect, or because my struggles are over. I wrote it because I finally realized that waiting for perfection waiting for a time when everything is easy and painless is the greatest trap of all.

For a long time, I thought the phrase "If it has to be, it's up to me" was a battle cry. I thought it meant fighting the world, carrying the weight of every outcome on my shoulders, and forcing my way to the top.

But after all the miles traveled, the prayers offered, and the quiet moments staring at the ceiling, I now know it means something much gentler.

It simply means taking ownership of your own peace.

It means having the grace to forgive yourself when you fail. It means looking at the people who love you ,your parents, your friends, your mentors and deciding to make them proud. It means trusting the divine flow of the universe enough to surrender the results, while still having the quiet courage to start your engine every single day.

We are all just travelers trying to find our way. I don't know where your road will take you after you close this book, and I don't know exactly where my own map will lead me next. But I know this: it is a beautiful privilege to simply be on the journey.

Thank you for sharing your most precious resource your **TIME** with me.

Wherever you are right now, take a deep breath. Forgive your past. Protect your peace.

The road is waiting. Step forward and make the promise to yourself: If it has to be, it's up to me.

- Hardik H Rane

A Final Note on Brotherhood: The Trimurti

They say that medical college teaches you about textbooks, but it is the people around you who teach you about life.

As I close this book, there are two people who deserve their own space on these pages. For the last four years, I have never had to walk alone. Through every single up and down, through the stress of exams, the heavy days of doubt, and the late-night overthinking, I always had two hands securely resting on my shoulders.

To my two gems, my roommates: we came as Goa boys navigating life in Karnataka, but we built a brotherhood that will last a lifetime. We are the "Three Murthys." You saw me at my absolute lowest, and you stood by me until I found my footing again.

Thank you for carrying my weight when I was tired, and for being the family I needed away from home. I only hope that throughout these four years, I was able to keep up to the mark and be the brother you both deserved.

I am forever grateful to you both. This journey is yours, too.